glory-us

A 40 Day Journey *for* Female-Identifying Folk

Jody Tucker

ILLUMIFY
MEDIA.COM

glory-us

Copyright © 2023 by Jody Tucker

Published by
Illumify Media Global
www.IllumifyMedia.com
"Let's bring your book to life!"

Paperback ISBN: 978-1-959099-18-5

Typeset by Art Innovations (http://artinnovations.in/)
Cover design by Debbie Lewis

Printed in the United States of America

CONTENTS

FOREWORD

$\mathcal{T}$his devotional, *Glory-Us* emerged from the deepest part of Jody Tucker's heart and her life's experiences. Jody's vulnerable transparency within these pages offers an authenticity showing that Jody understands both the joys women experience, as well as the painful experiences women have faced in their lives. She understands—she gets it!

Jody does not dwell on the negatives that we pass through in life, neither does she ignore them. Instead, she eloquently draws the reader to consider this truth. *Life's circumstances cannot redefine God's vision of who you are as a woman.* Herein lays the truth from which women can draw strength, hope, purpose, and vision; to see them as God's beautiful creation.

Jody concludes each day's devotional with poignant questions. These are not to be answered quickly. Allow the answer—your honest and unguarded answer—to rise up within you. This may take more time, but the result of your patience will become a treasured keepsake.

I have known Jody for many years. At first just from afar, but in the last few years I have come to know Jody personally as a woman after God's own heart. I have journeyed with Jody through overwhelming emotional tidal waves that she believed were certain to devour her; through turbulent rapids that convinced her she would be humiliated or left all alone; and then into new pastures of green where she would discover and learn the value of the gift she was being given: peace, rest, healing, hope, joy, love, and abundant life.

The devotional *Glory-Us* is not an answer book to life but a written opportunity for you, the reader, to explore, to reflect, to contemplate that in *all* things God's love and presence is a constant. The Spirit of God did not lie to you when these words were inspired to be written, "I will never leave you nor forsake you." Every single word is true. God goes with you into whatever you face in your life and will woo you to follow, but the Spirit of God will never abandon you or leave you high and dry.

As you navigate each new day, allow the words that God has placed on Jody's heart and mind to speak to you. Some days her words will speak louder and penetrate deeper into your own experience. Leave judgment at the door that something is or is not happening. Just as Jody discovered *something* is always happening you will too, because this is the source of spiritual momentum, healing, and freedom.

Abundant blessings to you as you enter this journey with *Glory-Us*.

Faith Donaldson,
Spiritual director, counselor,
soul journeyer, and seeker

INTRODUCTION

Sweet Sister,

*T*hank you for picking up this book. Reading these pages is one of a million little choices you are making consciously or unconsciously that will lead you on your path to discovering and unveiling more of the beautiful person you are created to be.

Many women hear the teachings of their mothers, grandmothers, leaders, and teachers and accept them without question. Some rebel from their elders and openly rebuke what they perceive as frameworks of oppression passed from generation to generation about our traditions and culturally specific roles as daughters, wives, and mothers. While others have experienced abuse or abandonment from the women we depended on to lead, nurture, and protect us. Regardless of our varied personal experiences, many of us feel something is missing altogether. We yearn for a collective and individual spiritual walk that is intimate and deep and in tune with the sweet voice of a loving and affirming Creator, but we often struggle to hear that voice above the noise of our lives, our losses, and sometimes even each other.

It is my hope that we can come together in and through these pages. We are created to be in deep fellowship and communion as fellow women, yet we bear the scars of our imperfect relationships. Many of us have become our own worst enemies, divided sharply along political and religious stances. We are our greatest resource, yet in many cases we have turned against ourselves. Where we should find our greatest strength, unity, and solidarity, we often either lash out in judgment, or pull back to avoid tiptoeing around our minefield of collective self-destruction.

It is my desire that through these pages you will find healing and hope. Each daily devotional begins with an inspired word representing the heart of God speaking to the you, followed by a daily scripture and collective prayer. The corresponding questions are meant as a starting place to prompt your own meditation, inspiration, and personal reflection. This practice requires you to be brave. Depending on your personal experiences, some questions might be more difficult to process than others. I desire that you feel the freedom and joy to fully become who you are uniquely created to be. I desire for you to embrace and engage with the beautifully dynamic and diverse community of women around the world who are here to walk alongside you. I desire for all of us to tap into the wisdom of our ancestors, as well as the keen insights of our daughters and granddaughters. Most importantly, I desire for you to know you are not alone, though you may have been made to believe you are.

So join me and become a part of the worldwide community of sisters who are on one another's side.

"Thus says God, the LORD,

who created the heavens and stretched them out,

who spread out the earth and what comes from it,

who gives breath to the people upon it

and spirit to those who walk in it:

I am the LORD; I have called you in righteousness;

I have taken you by the hand and kept you;

I have given you as a covenant to the people,

a light to the nations,   ·

to open the eyes that are blind,

to bring out the prisoners from the dungeon,

from the prison those who sit in darkness."

—ISAIAH 42:5-7

DAY 1

You Are Never Alone

My Glorious Ones,

You are concerned with many things. You wonder about the right thing to do. You are always thinking about what is best for others. But even if for just a moment, put everything aside and focus on me. Remember that I am with you. You are never alone. Even in your darkest moments, I am there. In the pain no one can witness, I am there. In the joy you feel that no one else can know, I am there. In your secret moments and during your celebrations, hardships, fears, and losses, I am with you wherever you go. I am the perfect Father, the perfect Mother, the perfect Sibling and friend. I am the family you always wanted. In my presence, you will find your hope and your strength. I will never push you away. I am here for you always. More than anything else, I want you to know and receive the love I have for you. You are perfect to me in every way, and I delight and rejoice in your presence.

A WORD FOR TODAY

"Here is my servant, whom I uphold,

my chosen, in whom my soul delights;

I have put my spirit upon her;

she will bring forth justice to the nations."

—ISAIAH 42:1 (AUTHOR'S PARAPHRASE)

TODAY'S PRAYER

Dear God,

Help us to know and seek your presence so that love can drive our service. Let us know how you would have us treat those around us. Also, provide us wisdom as we discern what treatment we should and should not condone for ourselves and our sisters. Give us hearts for justice, and help us to spread a message of your love, freedom, power, strength, and grace. Help all of your daughters across Earth to know they are powerful, seen, known, important, and loved.

In your secret moments and during your celebrations, hardships, fears, and losses, I am with you wherever you go.

QUESTIONS FOR REFLECTION

1. Do I believe in the deepest places of my spirit, soul, mind, heart, and body that I am loved, adored, and uniquely wonderful and beautiful? Why or why not?

    _____

    _____

    _____

    _____

2. How do I let my sisters of the world know, through my words and my actions, how beautiful and wonderful and loved they are?

    _____

    _____

    _____

    _____

DAY 2

Do Not Be Bridled

My Glorious Ones,

Today is a new day. I come to you with a new word that is fresh and just for you. I see you! I see your heart and your mind and your spirit and your body. I rejoice and delight in everything that you are! Your life is unique. You are known by me, and I am known by you. Yet the many competing voices in the world sometimes make you forget the truth of your value. Take a moment to look at the beauty of my creation, and remember that I make no mistakes. I have uniquely created you, which amounts to perfection in my eyes. Do not be led astray by the voices of others who want you to be something else in order to assuage their own egos and insecurities. My voice is the only one that will lead you to me.

A WORD FOR TODAY

"I will instruct you and teach you the way you should go;

I will counsel you with my eye upon you."

—PSALM 32:8

TODAY'S PRAYER

Dear God,

Help us to love ourselves as you love us. Restore in us all that has been robbed by the powers and worldviews that seek to steal, kill, and destroy. Renew us and lead us into a sacred place. Allow us to come directly to you to be nurtured at the Source. Help us to remind each other of that love and of our beauty. Free us from all that constrains us and controls us and keeps us from being able to run freely in your presence. Let us sing and dance and be filled with hope. Help us to not bridle one another or be dominated by the bits that others want to place in our mouths. Let us repent of our egotistical needs to judge or control our sisters in order to feel better about ourselves. Let us gallop without fences toward the freedom and joy you have prepared for us individually and collectively.

My voice is the only one that will lead you to me.

QUESTIONS FOR REFLECTION

1. How might the insecurities I feel about myself impact the way I relate to other
    women?

    _____

    _____

    _____

    _____

    _____

2. Do I feel completely free to be my unique and wonderful self? Why or why
    not?

    _____

    _____

    _____

    _____

DAY 3

Run to Me

My Glorious Ones,

D o you have any idea how much I love you? Do you have any idea how precious you are to me? I wish you could feel and know even the smallest particle of my love. It would be enough to restore you and sustain you and fill you with life. Though you might have become blind to my presence, busied by your own agendas, I still surround you and fill you. I go before you and behind you. I am with you and within you. Do not be troubled or afraid. Nothing you have done or said or thought or wondered will ever rob you of my love. Don't hide from me or distract yourself from me. My desire is to be with you and bless you and fill you with my spirit. Hear my voice in the birdsong at dawn. Feel my breath as the wind whistles through the trees. See my face in the unfolding flower. Through these natural offerings, know that you are never alone.

A WORD FOR TODAY

"I have swept away your transgressions like a cloud
and your sins like mist;
return to me, for I have redeemed you."

—ISAIAH 44:22

TODAY'S PRAYER

Dear God,

Help us bask in acceptance and grace. Help us accept the love that you have for us and for all of your children. We find refuge in the shadow of your wings. In this safe place, we are renewed and restored. Wrapped within your protective embrace, we make peace with ourselves, with each other, and with you. As you hold us within your sacred wings, your spirit allows us to receive the life and love and promise that was secured for us before the beginning of time. In this space, we can feel the warmth of your chest and feel your heart beating. In your presence, we are healed. You bring dawn to our darkness, and in a moment a new day is upon us. You set us back on our feet. Let mercy and forgiveness pour over us like a waterfall. Let us be an outpouring of mercy and forgiveness toward everyone we encounter or consider today.

Nothing you have done or said or thought or wondered will ever rob you of my love.

QUESTIONS FOR REFLECTION

1. What would my life be like if I woke up in the morning feeling completely free from every mistake I've ever made?

   _____

   _____

   _____

   _____

   _____

2. How would it feel to put self-loathing and self-judgment behind me?

   _____

   _____

   _____

   _____

   _____

3. How would my relationships with other women be transformed if I became a
    champion of mercy, grace, love, and unconditional positive regard for others?

    _____

    _____

    _____

    _____

    _____

DAY 4

I See You

My Glorious Ones,

You *are not invisible. I see you and know you during your difficult moments: The disappointment you felt when you made a bid for connection that wasn't returned. The rejection you felt when you thought someone rolled their eyes at you. The fear you felt when you didn't know how you were being perceived. The beautiful gesture you made that was ignored. The fears and insecurities that you hold deep in your heart, as well as the gifts that bubble up, ready to burst forth from inside of you. I see everything in real time. I acknowledge you. I validate you. And I have given you a voice. Use your voice, and speak your truth. Do not suppress your feelings. I give you specific insights and emotions for a reason. Stop feeling discounted by others. I am on your side, and I will always show up for you. But I also want you to show up for yourself. Stop being a silent martyr. Others can't see you if you refuse to see yourself. I don't make beautiful things for them to be hidden or diminished.*

A WORD FOR TODAY

"Creation itself will be set free from its enslavement to decay and will obtain the freedom of the glory of the children of God."

—ROMANS 8:21

TODAY'S PRAYER

Dear God,

Help us to feel empowered to use our voices. You have given each of us wisdom and strength and power, but sometimes we are consumed with our doubts. Let us not be afraid to live our lives out loud, supporting one another to be our fullest and truest selves, whatever that looks like.

Others can't see you if you refuse to see yourself.

QUESTIONS FOR REFLECTION

1. Which friends, family members, or colleagues demonstrate an ability to listen intently and validate what I say in a way that helps me feel truly heard?

_____

_____

_____

_____

_____

2. What are the attributes and qualities of these listeners?

_____

_____

_____

_____

_____

3. Do I have a healthy balance between being a good listener and honestly sharing my own perspective?

_____

_____

_____

_____

_____

_____

DAY 5

Find a New Path

My Glorious Ones,

J see you wanting to honor your relationships. But are you honoring me and the wisdom I have placed within your spirit? Are you honoring yourself and the voice you have been given? When you allow yourself to be silenced by the more dominant voices in your world, you not only perpetuate the silencing, you empower the wrong paradigm. I have created all of my children in my image, bearing both my powerful strength and my everlasting compassion. And just as no one is created to be enslaved, no one should feel forced to be an authority over another. All of my children need release from the hierarchical power structure that humans have created for themselves, as this is not my way. I am a lover and a dreamer—a holder of hands and hearts. Stop agonizing over who is in charge. Instead, choose to be in communion and in union with one another. Lead my children toward a more loving way. Be your fullest self, but also accept the authentic selves of those whom you love. Speak truth, and believe in the depths of your soul that a new day is dawning. Do not submit your authority over your heart or your body, and never surrender your voice. True love and partnership will never ask you to do that. Whatever you do, maintain your own integrity and know that sometimes the most loving thing you can do for others is walk away from what is unhealthy in order to love yourself.

A WORD FOR TODAY

"I will repay you for the years

that the swarming locust has eaten,

the hopper, the destroyer, and the cutter,

my great army that I sent against you.

You shall eat in plenty and be satisfied

and praise the name of the LORD your God,

who has dealt wondrously with you.

And my people shall never again be put to shame.

You shall know that I am in the midst of Israel

and that I, the LORD, am your God and there is no other.

And my people shall never again be put to shame."

—JOEL 2:25-29

TODAY'S PRAYER

Dear God,

Forgive us for putting new wine in old wineskins. You have empowered your children, but we choose cultural frameworks that hinder your spirit and diminish those we love. Let us experience true communion and oneness with one another. Let us be fully open to receiving gifts from the people you have put in our lives. Help transform us so that we can offer safety to one another, reminding us that we belong to each other. Deliver us quickly from the relationships that demand we be any less than who you have created us to be.

I have created all of my children in my image, bearing both my powerful strength and my everlasting compassion.

QUESTIONS FOR REFLECTION

1. How am I nurturing and creating safety and belonging in my relationships (for both myself and for others)?

    _____

    _____

    _____

    _____

    _____

2. Am I able to be my fullest self with the people around me? Are others able to be their fullest self with me?

    _____

    _____

    _____

    _____

    _____

DAY 6

See with New Eyes

My Glorious Ones,

You have made a lot of assumptions. You are not aware of how your unconscious framework impacts the way you see people. You don't see your own fear and defensiveness and self-protection. You don't realize that you have already made a judgment about what someone will say before they can open their mouth. You are jumping to conclusions instead of being a listener and a learner. I have compassion for you. I understand. I know that hurt can make your heart hard and your head race. You may have valid reasons to withhold your trust. But I want you to start breaking down your walls. I have many gifts for you, and sometimes I deliver them in unpredictable ways through unexpected people. Everyone has their own story. Let them tell it. You might be surprised.

A WORD FOR TODAY

"I do not call you servants any longer, because the servant does not know what the master is doing, but I have called you friends, because I have made known to you everything that I have heard from God. You did not choose me, but I chose you. And I appointed you to go and bear fruit, fruit that will last, so that God will give you whatever you ask in my name. I am giving you these commands so that you may love one another."

—JOHN 15:15-17 (AUTHOR'S PARAPHRASE)

TODAY'S PRAYER

Dear God,

Help us remember that we are all connected to one another. When one rejoices, we all have cause to celebrate. When one hurts, we all suffer. Forgive us, Lord, for losing our communities, our connection, our collaboration, and our collective spirit. Teach us to live as a village. Show us how to care for one another and for all of the children and elders in our communities. Open our eyes to see the beauty of living in unity and open-heartedness instead of judgment and self-protection. Heal the wounds that have crafted cultures of competition and self-protection, thus leading us down paths of isolation. Help us rebuke the lies that make us believe we must carry our burdens alone. Graft us together in your love.

I have many gifts for you, and sometimes I deliver them in unpredictable ways through unexpected people

---

QUESTIONS FOR REFLECTION

1. How do I respond to other women who cause me to become defensive, shut down, or self-protective? Can I recognize the moments I have made others feel that way?

    _____

    _____

    _____

    _____

2. What messages can I proactively deliver, or what intentional actions can I take, to ensure that the important people in my life know I am on their side no matter what?

    _____

    _____

    _____

    _____

DAY 7

Asking for Help

My Glorious Ones,

I know when you are hurting. You face hardships you think no one else will understand. What gave you the impression that you are supposed to do this alone? When did shame first silence you? When did judgment from others first make you afraid? I have given you the greatest gift I could imagine on Earth: each other. When did you forget you are all on the same team? You are afraid to tell your story and speak honestly. Yet the worst possible thing for you is isolation. Many others are experiencing the same thing you are going through right now. It is arrogant to think you are the only one facing the battle that is before you. It is egotistical to believe you are the only one in this storm. Go public with your struggles. In being open and transparent, you may find the strength and resources you need today. Your honesty might also be the lighthouse in the storm that shows others where to find the shore.

A WORD FOR TODAY

"And the one who sent me is with me; God has not left me alone."

—JOHN 8:29 (AUTHOR'S PARAPHRASE)

TODAY'S PRAYER

Dear God,

Remind us of those who are on our side. Give us the courage to reach out and connect. Help us to be available and approachable and interruptible when we are the ones who are called. Let us call out the courage in one another that allows us to speak without fear of rejection or judgment or condemnation. Pour over us your spirit so that we might engage with honesty and authenticity and vulnerability. Let us lock arms with one another as we walk forward on our individual and collective paths.

I have given you the greatest gift I could imagine on Earth: each other.

QUESTIONS FOR REFLECTION

1. Do I feel comfortable being totally honest with my closest friends? If not, how
    can I take steps to open up and share more of myself?

    _____

    _____

    _____

    _____

2. Do I have people in my life who make it safe for me to be honest and
    authentic? If not, how might I cultivate these relationships? If yes, how can I
    go deeper with these friends?

    _____

    _____

    _____

    _____

DAY 8

Do Justly, Love Mercy, and Walk Humbly

My Glorious Ones,

So many of your sisters are trying to stay alive in the middle of a stormy sea. All of their energy is spent keeping themselves afloat. They are never far from drowning. Every breath is a struggle for air. They are either continually pushed beneath the surface by those in power, or they are coupled to anchors that threaten to pull them under. Even when they look okay, they are not okay. You have within you the power to help rescue them. You can be a lifeboat that rows them to shore. Yet many times, you have unknowingly summoned them to death. Every time you told your sister that love perseveres, that love endures, that love conquers all, you failed to see the chains you may have wrapped around her flailing arms. When you ignored the bruises on her soul and told her prayer is the answer, you may have sentenced her to death. When you posted that meme—"Bloom Where You Are Planted"—you may have ignored or been unaware that she was wedged in the crack of an active volcano. When you made the conversation political instead of personal, you may have led her to believe that both you and your ideas about God are unsafe. Every time you talked more than you listened . . . Every time you didn't ask questions or thought you had the answers . . . Every time you decided it was none of your business . . . you might have denied her the chance to ask you for help. There might have been good in your intentions, but maybe she didn't need to be told how to be more loving or faithful or fruitful. Maybe she needed someone to open the prison doors, walk into her cell, and lead her out.

A WORD FOR TODAY

"God has told you, O mortal, what is good,
and what does the Lord require of you
but to do justice and to love kindness
and to walk humbly with your God?"

—MICAH 6:8 (AUTHORS PARAPHRASE)

TODAY'S PRAYER

Dear God,

Please help us to be merciful and kind to one another. Place on our hearts the needs of our sisters around the globe. Create in us a worldwide community of compassion and love. Rise up in us a righteous anger to fight for justice for those among us who are enslaved, oppressed, and marginalized. Rescue those among us who are being abused physically, emotionally, psychologically, sexually, or spiritually. Remove our blinders to the ways we are complicit in allowing your daughters to be treated as second-class citizens or, in some places, treated as non-citizens. Make us aware of our unconscious bias, societal arrogance, and spiritual pride. Help us repent and turn toward you in humility. Let us serve one another without flinching and fight for every sister as if she were our own daughter.

Maybe she needed someone to open the prison doors, walk into her cell, and lead her out.

QUESTIONS FOR REFLECTION

1. Has my commitment to my own way of thinking ever caused me to act
    without love, mercy, or compassion?

    _____

    _____

    _____

    _____

2. How might each of us "walking humbly with our God" create a more just
    society for us all?

    _____

    _____

    _____

    _____

DAY 9

Feel It All; Honor It All

My Glorious Ones,

*I desire that you would lean into me and trust me with your whole self.
I desire for your heart, mind, spirit, soul, and body to come awake and feel
alive. In so many ways you have numbed yourself. You have told yourself what
is acceptable and unacceptable to feel. You have created rules around what is
godly and holy and righteous. Therefore you have denied your anger. You have
denied your resentments. You have denied your wounds and have prayed to have
everything you see as a negative emotion transformed into love and mercy and
service. But love and mercy and service flow from wholeness, and you cannot
be whole if you deny your feelings. Let them come up. Let them swirl over you,
around you, and then release them. Acknowledge and feel your full range of
emotions, and do not carry shame for a single one. Trust your body, your heart,
your soul, and your spirit to tell you things that your mind may or may not
comprehend. You are as complex and beautiful as the ocean. Let every wave
come, no matter how gentle or aggressive. From my perspective, every experience
you have flows in perfect balance, in and out. You were not meant to keep
anything in, so feel it all and honor it all.*

A WORD FOR TODAY

"How long, O Lord? Will you forget me forever?

How long will you hide your face from me?

How long must I bear pain in my soul

and have sorrow in my heart all day long?

How long shall my enemy be exalted over me?

Consider and answer me, O Lord my God!

Give light to my eyes, or I will sleep the sleep of death,

and my enemy will say, 'I have prevailed';

my foes will rejoice because I am shaken.

But I trusted in your steadfast love;

my heart shall rejoice in your salvation.

I will sing to the Lord

because God has dealt bountifully with me."

—PSALM 13 (AUTHOR'S PARAPHRASE)

TODAY'S PRAYER

Dear God,

Allow us to feel and honor the fullness of our human experience. Allow us to have grace for ourselves and for one another. Help us see one another as sisters instead of foes to be feared. Help us dispel the lies that make us believe others might rejoice when we fall. Show us our unconscious biases and prejudices that cause us to judge each other instead of circling around one another in protection and unity. Come alongside us as we receive your love and mercy, even in our imperfections, so that we stop pretending to be righteous. Heal us from all the ways we have been intentionally and unintentionally divided against each other. Remind us that we are daughters, sisters, mothers, and blessed companions in our struggles.

Trust your body, your heart, your soul, and your spirit to tell you things that your mind may or may not comprehend.

QUESTIONS FOR REFLECTION

1. Do I allow myself to feel all of my emotions, or are there some emotions that I suppress or feel shame about?

    _____

    _____

    _____

    _____

2. Do I allow my sisters to express all of their emotions, or does that make me uncomfortable?

    _____

    _____

    _____

    _____

Shame Is a Liar

My Glorious Ones,

*Y*ou are beginning to see and know and understand that shame is a lie. Shame is the enemy that keeps you from receiving whole and perfect love. Shame also keeps you from being fully known by one another. You know in the depths of your being that shame is not from me, yet still you hold onto your secrets. You may have been told that you need to be saved or rescued, as if I desire for you to be transformed into someone or something different. Remember, I created you intentionally. I love you so deeply and want nothing more than for you to receive my love. I formed you. I love you. I delight in you. I long more than anything for you to let me lavish my love upon you. I am a lover who desires to take you up in my arms and look deeply into your eyes. But when you attach shame onto your identity or you make another feel shameful, you are choosing to look away. Have I not done everything to show you that I long for you? Can you not see me surrounding you with the beauty of creation? Do you not hear me in the birdsong? Can you not feel me in the breeze, sending strokes of my loving-kindness? Do you still not fully understand that I would sacrifice everything to *ensure my communion with you? How else can I prove it to you? Turn from condemnation and shame. Return to me. I've made a beautiful world for us to live in together. I long to hold you, be with you, and love on you forever. Be released from your shame so that you might receive me into your full self. Take me deeply into you, and let my spirit move and pulse and create life within you. See and know and feel that my love for you is great.*

A WORD FOR TODAY

"The LORD, your God, is in your midst,

a warrior who gives victory;

God will rejoice over you with gladness;

God will renew you in love;

God will exult over you with loud singing."

—ZEPHANIAH 3:17 (AUTHOR'S PARAPHRASE)

TODAY'S PRAYER

Dear God,

To identify as female in this culture often has us feeling confused. We are confused about these beautiful bodies we are given and how to celebrate them, feel safe in them, know them, and respect them, especially in a world that dehumanizes and exploits physical beauty. It is as if we belong to everyone except ourselves. Help us reclaim ourselves and bask in the wonder of our beauty.

I long more than anything for you to let me lavish my love upon you.

QUESTIONS FOR REFLECTION

1. What would it be like to live in a world with no shame?

   _____

   _____

   _____

   _____

2. How would my perspective of myself and others change if I could only see beauty?

   _____

   _____

   _____

   _____

DAY 11

Walk Together

My Glorious Ones,

You need your sisters. You were created to connect and be heard and belong. There are times you want to talk but don't know what to say. There are times you wish you could tell your story, but you are not sure how to start. There are times you want to ask for help but don't want to be a burden. You are afraid that you will be judged. There are times that the words have tried to bubble up, and a sister unknowingly filled the space with small talk. There are times that you started to form the words and you were interrupted because your sister connected to what she thought you were going to say or was triggered by your words and needed to verbally process her own trauma. There are times when you dominated conversation instead of making space for a sister to be vulnerable with you. Regardless of the role you have played in conversations, all of these experiences have kept you hidden and small. They have stopped you from telling your story or asking for help. They have diminished your voice. Know that while not everyone is safe, many of your sisters are. Find them. Do not stop looking for them. Believe that they are there and ask me to show them to you. You deserve to be part of a loving and grace-filled community. You deserve to be heard and acknowledged and known, and to hear and acknowledge your sisters. You deserve to know that you belong to a deep, rich sisterhood. Find your people. Have grace for those who have not shown up for you the way you needed them to. They need their sisters too.

A WORD FOR TODAY

"I will lead the blind

by a road they do not know;

by paths they have not known

I will guide them.

I will turn the darkness before them into light,

the rough places into level ground.

These are the things I will do,

and I will not forsake them."

—ISAIAH 42:16

TODAY'S PRAYER

Dear God,

Humble our hearts that we may see your goodness. Quiet our minds so that we may know your peace. Help us make space for each other as we journey and to boldly step into the space that you create for us in our communities. Bring to us the connection and unity we so desperately long for.

**You deserve to be heard
and acknowledged and known.**

QUESTIONS FOR REFLECTION

1. Do I go about my plans and my to-do list with automaticity? If so, can I allow
    myself to stay open to whomever might walk into my world and need someone
    to talk to today?

    _____

    _____

    _____

    _____

    _____

2. Is there a person in my life that I can be open and honest with about my own
    struggles and insecurities? If not, is there a person in my life who I feel drawn
    to engage more deeply with?

    _____

    _____

    _____

    _____

Drink Deep

My Glorious Ones,

I see that your days are busy. I know that your burdens are heavy. I hear the cries of your soul when you lay down to rest. Let me assure you of something that you already know in your spirit: When you wholeheartedly serve those you love, you reap personal benefits and deep joy. But remember to stop when you are tired. Take notice when you feel resentment. Pay attention to your anger. While I do not want you to focus your energy on your fears or worries, I ask that you not ignore your feelings. These are signs that I send you to tell you something is out of balance. Ask your feelings what they would like to tell you. Then ask me to heal and restore you. I will. Drink deeply from the boundless and abundant waters I provide. You deserve more than sips from a stagnant and dead lake. Turn toward the people who will refresh you, restore you, and rejuvenate you today. Just as you might filter tap water to ensure the healthiest form of hydration, you may also need to filter toxic people from your life in order to receive pure refreshment for your soul. Drink deeply and intentionally from the well of life.

A WORD FOR TODAY

"Satisfy us in the morning with your steadfast love,

so that we may rejoice and be glad all our days."

—PSALM 90:14

TODAY'S PRAYER

Dear God,

Let us walk without fear as we seek your spirit. Let us hold nothing back as we follow after your truth. Let your life be revealed in us and through us. Pour over us your goodness and your kindness and your grace. Allow our deepest thirsts to be quenched. Satisfy us, cleanse us, and let your Spirit wash over us. Let us draw from the deepest wells and taste the sweetest of waters. Let us take it in ourselves and offer it to one another.

Drink deeply from the boundless and abundant waters I provide.

QUESTIONS FOR REFLECTION

1. Who around me seems to be "full" and "refreshed?" How can I learn more from them?

    _____

    _____

    _____

    _____

    _____

2. How can I increase the number and quality of relationships I have with people who are healthy and whole?

    _____

    _____

    _____

    _____

    _____

DAY 13

Stop Worrying About Worrying

My Glorious Ones,

You have been told again and again not to worry. You have been reminded over and over not to fear. Your sisters and teachers and ancestors have told you these things time and time again. Psychologists, authors, preachers, podcasters—and even Scripture—explain that faith, not fear, is the path to life. And yet, you still find yourself troubled and afraid, wondering why you can't overcome these powerful forces at work in your life. Hear me now: You will always be able to find something to worry about. Worrying is a natural experience of being human, of taking risks, and of loving. Accept your worries instead of fighting them or berating yourself for feeling them. But don't live in that place of angst. Notice these emotions thank them for speaking to you, and then let them go. Walk through the moment and get beyond it. Your concerns do not define you, but you cannot live into your fullest potential if you choose to stay safe and small. You will need to face your fears and anxieties instead of ignoring them or suppressing them to become who you are created to be. Your worries and fears are not the end of the story; they are a guide to help you stay reflective on your path. Do not let worry control you. Instead, listen to what your worries have to say and then ask for your loving Creator to step through it with you.

A WORD FOR TODAY

"Thus the LORD has shown the mercy promised to our ancestors

and has remembered God's holy covenant,

the oath that God swore to our ancestor Abraham,

to grant us that we, being rescued from the hands of our enemies,

might serve the LORD without fear, in holiness and righteousness

in God's presence all our days."

—LUKE 1:72–75 (AUTHOR'S PARAPHRASE)

TODAY'S PRAYER

Dear God,

Help us not focus so much on what not to do. Lead us toward a vision of what we can have in your Spirit. Ground us in your power and in your truth. Show us the life and love that is available to us. Dispel our disbeliefs. Displace our doubts. Fill us with such overwhelming wonder and love for life that there is room for little else. Teach us how to truly connect with one another so that we can be gently shaken out of our tunneled, egocentric focus. Show us what to celebrate and teach us to dance.

Your concerns do not define you, but you cannot live into your fullest potential if you choose to stay safe and small.

QUESTIONS FOR REFLECTION

1. What control do I have over the things that are creating fear in my life?

    _____

    _____

    _____

    _____

    _____

2. Do I spend a lot of energy thinking about and analyzing my worries? What would happen if I spent that energy identifying and moving toward what I want instead of focusing on what I am afraid might happen?

    _____

    _____

    _____

    _____

DAY 14

Drink Deep from the Wellspring of Peace

My Glorious Ones,

Look up! See the light of a new dawn. See the beauty in the clouds. See how the tree branches, twisted and tangled as they are, continue to shoot up toward the sky. Everything is changing at every moment. A canvas is being painted before your very eyes. Feel the wind brush against your skin. Smell how the season is changing ever so slightly. A mighty production is taking place, a symphony for your senses. Breathe in deeply my beauty. Breathe in deeply my love. Take notice and cherish every little thing.

A WORD FOR TODAY

"And you, child, will be called the prophet of the Most High,

for you will go before the Lord to prepare God's ways,

to give God's people knowledge of salvation

by the forgiveness of their sins.

Because of the tender mercy of our God,

the dawn from on high will break upon us,

to shine upon those who sit in darkness and in the shadow of death,

to guide our feet into the way of peace."

—LUKE 1:76-79 (AUTHOR'S PARAPHRASE)

TODAY'S PRAYER

Dear God,

Guide our feet toward the path of peace. Let us be a beacon for our sisters to guide them toward indescribable beauty and unexplainable joy. Let your tender mercy infiltrate our bodies, hearts, and minds so that we can travel together in harmony toward what is fresh and alive and true. Do not let us gather by or drink from stagnant lakes; instead, lead us to places that will nurture and nourish us. Show us where to find the wells that draw up from the true and deep source—the wells that overflow with pure spring water. Guide us down the paths that will lead us toward the peace you will make known to us and pour out over us.

Breathe in deeply my beauty.
Breathe in deeply my love.

QUESTIONS FOR REFLECTION

1. What type of margin do I build into my life for communion with nature? For communion with others? For communion with God?

    _____

    _____

    _____

    _____

    _____

2. Do my sisters see me as approachable and interruptible, or do I appear too busy to be bothered? Does my schedule allow others access to me on their time, or only on my time?

    _____

    _____

    _____

    _____

DAY 15

Move Beyond Yourself

My Glorious Ones,

Today is the day to reach out. Whatever you are facing, there is a sister ready and able to journey with you and help carry your load. Your burdens can be shared. Whatever overwhelms or discourages you can be managed better with a friend at your side. There is a sister ready to hold space for your heart. There is a sister ready to catch your tears. There is a sister ready to share a meal or go for a drive or help with your household chores. Do not believe the lie that you are alone. Whatever joys you are feeling can be shared and will then bless others. You can share the celebration that you think no one cares about. You can express your gratitude and verbalize your dreams. You can speak your truth and fuel the fire of your passions. Whatever reality you show up in today, choose to engage in communion and unity to expand or fortify your community. Move beyond your ego and the perception you are trying to create in order to invite others into the reality you are facing today.

A WORD FOR TODAY

"I lift up my eyes to the hills—

from where will my help come?

My help comes from the LORD,

who made heaven and earth.

God will not let your foot be moved;

The LORD who keeps you will not slumber.

The One who keeps Israel

will neither slumber nor sleep;

The LORD is your keeper;

the LORD is your shade at your right hand.

The sun shall not strike you by day

nor the moon by night.

The LORD will keep you from all evil;

God will keep your life.

The LORD will keep

your going out and your coming in

from this time on and forevermore."

—PSALM 121 (AUTHOR'S PARAPHRASE)

TODAY'S PRAYER

Dear God,

You are an ever-present Guide to lead us. Help us to find our helpers. Keep us in safety and remind us we are never alone.

Do not believe the lie that you are alone.

QUESTIONS FOR REFLECTION

1. Which of my sisters in my contact list would do anything to help me if I asked?

    _____

    _____

    _____

    _____

    _____

2. Can my sisters trust me to be full of grace, love, and support no matter what they are going through?

    _____

    _____

    _____

    _____

    _____

3. Would my social media posts and/or vocalized opinions create hesitation or prevent my sisters from approaching me in their time of need?

_____

_____

_____

_____

_____

DAY 16

Pass Through

My Glorious Ones,

Some boast about the difficulties in their jobs or marriages or other relationships as if they think their perseverance through trials makes them better equipped to experience my grace and love. While it is true that I meet you in the midst of your pain, I do not require it in order to develop a more intimate relationship with you. While it is true that you can grow from your challenges, I do not desire for you to be placed in difficult circumstances in order that you develop more fully into who I am creating you to be. No, it is quite the opposite. I long to lavish love on you and for you to find spaces with people who do the same. You have told yourself some pretty gruesome lies in order to live with the choices you have made, and you perpetuate this rhetoric. Many of your sisters are with people who are not good for them. Many live in toxic, unhealthy, or abusive situations. And yet their sisters somehow paint this as holy? Please know that I do not desire self-betrayal on your part. I desire for you to thrive. I showed myself as a sacrifice for the world. Would you ignore this gift? Do you think you and your sisters deserve to be punished? Punishment is never my will. Yes, you can find great joy in surrender. But I never asked you to be in harm's way.

A WORD FOR TODAY

"When you pass through the waters, I will be with you,

and through the rivers, they shall not overwhelm you;

when you walk through fire you shall not be burned,

and the flame shall not consume you."

—ISAIAH 43:2

TODAY'S PRAYER

Dear God,

You promise to be with us as we walk through fires and pass through floods. You promise that we will never be swept away or set ablaze. We trust you to be with us in every circumstance. Help us to know when to stay and when to walk away. Guide us when it is time to reach higher ground. Help us keep moving toward you, which always leads to a path of freedom, love, and life. Let us see clearly the partners and friends who lift us up. Let us also see clearly those who consciously or unconsciously are heaping more upon us. Let us walk our paths with courage. Let us have grace for one another. Keep us from judgment and shame so that we might be more open to tell one another our truths and rescue one another from harmful environments.

While it is true that I meet you in the midst of your pain, I do not require it in order to develop a more intimate relationship with you.

QUESTIONS FOR REFLECTION

1. Do I believe that I need to endure hardships in order to grow? If yes, how can I begin to remove this untruth?

_____

_____

_____

_____

2. If I were to follow my bliss, where might it lead me?

_____

_____

_____

_____

DAY 17

Gallop

My Glorious Ones,

I *know you wake each day with a busy mind, considering all that needs to be done. You are driven toward fulfilling many purposes and meeting many needs in this life you have chosen. You know there are times you must slow down and pay attention to all of the ways that I surround you with love and life and pleasure. You may choose to slow down today and rest in my presence. I am always ready to create space for your needs to be met. But you also can choose to run fervently toward the tasks set before you. I am there too. I am in you and before you and behind you. I have placed in your heart the unique passions that propel you. You are never escaping me, even when you pour yourself into your work or your relationships. Take notice of me. Your drive is one of the gifts I have emboldened you with. Pour yourself passionately into whatever your day has for you to create. Certainly, I am driven for my creation as well, and you are made in my image. Keep your ear tuned to my voice; we can tackle your list together.*

A WORD FOR TODAY

"We always give thanks to God
for all of you and mention you in our prayers,
constantly remembering before our God
your work of faith and labor of love
and steadfastness of hope
in our Lord Jesus Christ."

**—1 THESSALONIANS 1:2-3
(AUTHOR'S PARAPHRASE)**

TODAY'S PRAYER

Dear God,

Help us celebrate the path we are walking today. Fill us with your energy, inspiration, and passion. Let us embrace the unique opportunities that you give each of us. Forgive us for becoming divided by our need to overthink our own choices and our sisters' paths. Forgive us for believing the lies of our culture. We do not have conflicting priorities. Our careers and ministries and families are not in competition for our attention. We are not rooted in rivalry, vying against one another to stay out of last place. Help us embrace the rich and complex lives at work, at home, and in our communities. Help us to gather together at your effervescent trough. Fill us with individual and collective strength, power, and beauty. Let us collectively reject the idea that life is a race to be won. Give us the joy of experiencing this exciting journey that quickens our heartbeats and causes the wind to rush through our hair. Help us to gallop as a breathtaking herd over your beautiful wilderness like wild and free horses. Remind us that we are not racing against each other. There are no lanes. Set us free from the circles we run around, and remind us how to gallop across open land. Shake the earth with the thunder from our hooves.

I have placed in your heart
the unique passions that propel you.

QUESTIONS FOR REFLECTION

1. Am I aware of the deep and unique gifts, insights, power, strength, motivations, and creativity that drive, inspire, and empower me?

   _____

   _____

   _____

   _____

   _____

2. Am I "running a race" that has been created for me by others? Could I be the one creating a race for others to run?

   _____

   _____

   _____

   _____

   _____

DAY 18

Arise

My Glorious Ones,

$\mathcal{Y}$*ou have gotten so many mixed messages about your physical body and sensual nature. It is as if the whole world feels entitled to voice opinions about how you look, what you wear, and the choices you make. You've been depleted by the demands and critiques of the culture. Sadly, much of this damage has been done in the name of God! Have you shut down any part of yourself as a result? Have you detached in order to survive the verbal, visual, and physical assaults of misogynistic, misled men? Have you created or adopted a narrative that rationalizes their behavior? Deep inside, you wrestle and writhe because you know you are not a product to be consumed. Your nervous system is always on alert, whether you notice it or not, scanning for threats and attempting to keep you safe. Your analytical and judgmental mind overrides your body, and for good reason! The walls you have put up to protect yourself are justified! Take notice of these things so you can begin to heal. Reject what has been, then move toward a way of being that is aligned with your deepest innate knowing. A new way is unfolding. A rebirth of the feminine is upon us. See yourself with new eyes. You are beautiful and brilliant in every way. Every curve of your body, or lack thereof. Every inch of your skin. Each delicate facial feature. I delight in how you are made. Reclaim both your sexuality and your holiness. These things do not live on a continuum. You are a combination of these attributes all the time. Be fully awake and fully alive. Wholeheartedly pursue your passion. Debunk shame and self-loathing. Do not let yourself be diminished by those who are threatened by the marvelous mystery that is beheld in your beautiful body.*

A WORD FOR TODAY

"My beloved speaks and says to me:

'Arise, my love, my fair one,

and come away,

for now the winter is past,

the rain is over and gone.

The flowers appear on the earth;

the time of singing has come,

and the voice of the turtledove

is heard in our land.

The fig tree puts forth its figs,

and the vines are in blossom;

they give forth fragrance.

Arise, my love, my fair one,

and come away.'"

—SONG OF SONGS 2:10-13

TODAY'S PRAYER

Dear God,

We have walked afraid, but we have nothing to fear. The power that is in us and among us as a sisterhood of women is stronger than anything that has ever tried to overcome us, demoralize us, or diminish us. Strengthen us in unity against our oppressors and abusers. Heal our hearts so that we can be whole and holy. Reunite us as a broader body of believers. Give us the courage to lead one another into a new dawn for ourselves, and for our children.

See yourself with new eyes.
You are beautiful and brilliant in every way.

QUESTIONS FOR REFLECTION

1. What false stories have I believed about myself and my body?

   _____

   _____

   _____

   _____

2. What new narratives are unfolding? What new narratives would I like to bring to life?

   _____

   _____

   _____

   _____

DAY 19

Embrace Your Unique Beauty

My Glorious Ones,

*S*ome of you were taught by the generations before you that there is a "right" path and a proper way to be, to act, and to live. Believing this to be true, you looked for signposts along the way to illuminate your journey and to affirm you were headed in the right direction. In this paradigm, you sought validation from others that you perceived were on a similar path as you. If you believe the lie of pursuing human righteousness, you are in bondage to weighing every thought and behavior on some invisible scale. But there is no scale, no comparative weight, no normative measures. You are not the sum of what others have judged you to be. Do not perpetuate the lies that lead you and others toward clone-making behaviors. See it and name it for what it is: a slap in the face of the one who delights in your uniqueness. Don't put limits on my creativity. I do not make anything or anyone who doesn't reflect some aspect of my image, my characteristics, my attributes—including you. If you *must have examples, look to nature to be inspired. See yourself in the sun as it rises. See yourself in the river as it flows. Consider how the waves crash on the shore and the skies thunder with rain to nourish the land. See how animals play and how birds soar. You were made to rise above the constrictions and confinements of what you were taught to be. You are ready to live out the fullness of who you are.*

A WORD FOR TODAY

"I praise you, for I am fearfully and wonderfully made.

Wonderful are your works;

that I know very well."

—PSALM 139:14

TODAY'S PRAYER

Dear God,

Bring to our awareness all of the explicit and unconscious ways that we have been taught how to be. Help us to reject the lies of sameness, conformity, and cultural norming. Help us see how we have been dominated and oppressed by visible and invisible hierarchies that cause us to continue to live with bias and prejudice against one another and ourselves. Let us repent of the ways we have judged and distanced ourselves from one another. Make us lovers and appreciators of the entirety of your creation. All of the "isms" that plague our culture are rooted in our fear, judgment and misled needs to rationalize our own ways of being. Forgive us and help us to embrace each other. Help us to celebrate our deep dimensions of diversity, fully embracing and celebrating those who look, act, talk, believe, or love differently than us, knowing that through them we get to appreciate and behold a new aspect of you. We are all made in your glorious image.

You were made to rise above the constrictions and confinements of what you were taught to be.

QUESTIONS FOR REFLECTION

1. What are some of the characteristics, attributes, and descriptions of nature? How can I lean into these same descriptions as qualities that I possess? What actions can I take to nurture these attributes in myself?

   _____

   _____

   _____

   _____

2. Can I identify friends and role models who demonstrate nonjudgmental love, wholehearted acceptance, and unconditional positive regard for me and encourage me to be my unique self?

   _____

   _____

   _____

   _____

DAY 20

Be Free from Captivity

My Glorious Ones,

*B*ehold the beauty that lives within each of your sisters here on Earth. What a marvelous thing I have done! Each of you is so distinct from one another, and yet I delight in every one of you entirely. Your tendency has been to judge—to look for what is good or bad in others. Your own fears and rationalizations inhibit you from being able to gaze deeply into one another's souls where your true being resides. You stop with surface observations. But this has kept you from embracing other ways of knowing. You are held captive to your own beliefs, and your limited perception imprisons your sisters. Your polarization has robbed you of the rich funds of knowledge that are available and accessible only through people who are different from you. If you ask, I will reveal your unconscious biases to you. I desire for you to interrogate the frameworks that have surrounded you. They are not from me. Fall to your knees in humility and gratitude for all of humanity. Repent and return to me. Then rise in your strength and power to make way for a new way. Individually and collectively, debunk and deconstruct systems of oppression and marginalization. You were involuntarily born into it and unwittingly ascribe to it, but you shall take hold of it now.

A WORD FOR TODAY

"The spirit of the LORD GOD is upon me

because the LORD has anointed me;

God has sent me to bring good news to the oppressed,

to bind up the brokenhearted,

to proclaim liberty to the captives

and release to the prisoners."

—ISAIAH 61:1 (AUTHOR'S PARAPHRASE)

TODAY'S PRAYER

Dear God,

Forgive us for the ways we judge others. We repent of our conflict, dissension, and discord. Make us aware of the frameworks that created our unconscious beliefs. Purge us from perspectives that cause us to be divided and conquered. Give us grace for our sisters. Help us turn from prejudice and pride. Root us in strength and conviction, growing us to speak powerful truths to the world about the freedom and power we might inherit through your Spirit. Sing through us a mighty chorus.

Rise in your strength and power
to make way for a new way.

QUESTIONS FOR REFLECTION

1. What are some things that make me uniquely different from others around me?

    _____

    _____

    _____

    _____

2. Have I ever felt misunderstood or judged unfairly by someone? How did that make me feel?

    _____

    _____

    _____

    _____

DAY 21

Laugh Again

My Glorious Ones,

It is time to smile more. It is time to live out your joy. I would never ask you to ignore or deny your pain. Those deep inflictions on your heart allow you to feel deeply, love wholly, and live without regret. Do not ignore any of the feelings that present themselves to you throughout your day, especially the ones that remind you of your humanity. But be careful not to overanalyze yourself. Don't wallow there or spend your time and energy with people who weigh you down. Surround yourself with those who bring you light and life. It is time to find your laugh—the one that comes up deep from your belly and brings you to joyful tears.

A WORD FOR TODAY

"The thief comes only
to steal and kill and destroy.
I came that they may have life
and have it abundantly."

—JOHN 10:10

TODAY'S PRAYER

Dear God,

Help us to be like children again, filled with curiosity and wonder. Help us lose ourselves as we play in creek beds and stare at shape-shifting clouds in the sky. Pour love and joy over us so that we might feel complete, lacking nothing. Let us sing at the top of our lungs and run fervently through open fields. Let us taste our food and feel the sun on our face. Let us lie down and sleep in peace, then wake with a fresh and renewed spirit. Let our spirits soar in the knowledge of the love we were created to receive.

Surround yourself with those who bring you light and life.

QUESTIONS FOR REFLECTION

1. What kinds of things did I love to do as a child?

    _____

    _____

    _____

    _____

    _____

2. Can I remember how to play? What would that look like today?

    _____

    _____

    _____

    _____

    _____

DAY 22

Embrace Your Feelings

My Glorious Ones,

Begin to see all your feelings as friends. They are like welcome visitors who ring the bell at your front porch. As soon as you hear the sound, open the door to them. Invite them in. Sit down with them for a cup of tea and find out what wisdom and insight they have to share with you today. Don't ignore them. They will go around to the back door and knock incessantly throughout the day. If you still refuse to listen, they will simply come back tomorrow. Sit with them from the very start, give them some time, glean whatever you need from them, and then stand up and move about your day. Sometimes they will come with suitcases and ask to stay for a while. Other times, they will be gone as quickly as they came. Once you have heard what they want to tell you, you can choose whether to say goodbye and ask them to leave, or you can let them be your companions for a while longer. They need not overtake your life, yet they cannot be neglected. They are a gift. Don't try to explain or rationalize to anyone why they are there. They just are. They are not limited by the way they can be described with the words we have invented in our human language. They are a myriad of beautiful and complex reflections of your soul, your being, your human experience. They are rich and deep and pure and were never meant to be used against you the insight of your emotions threatens those who need to protect their own egos. Your empathic nature makes you rich and wise and strong. Your emotions peel the veneer off the surface and tell you about what is unseen. They offer a gentle and torrential way of knowing that cannot be duplicated or dominated. Reclaim them as your superpower! Feelings don't exist to be defended, excused, whisked away, or indulged. Feelings simply need to be felt. Tell each other what they have to say to you so that your sisters and daughters and granddaughters can easily recognize and welcome their voice as well.

A WORD FOR TODAY

"My mouth shall speak wisdom;

the meditation of my heart shall be understanding."

—PSALM 49:3

TODAY'S PRAYER

Dear God,

*Help us debunk the lies of our culture that tell us emotions make us weak.
Revive within us a desire to feel deeply without being afraid of judgment or
negative repercussions. Make us vulnerable, authentic, and fully alive. Help us
be brave and courageous enough to embrace our whole selves and one another's
feelings without denial, defensiveness, or destructive behaviors.*

Feelings simply need to be felt.

QUESTIONS FOR REFLECTION

1. What messages did I get from my family about emotions when I was a child?

_____

_____

_____

_____

_____

2. How do those messages enhance or inhibit my ability to feel my feelings today?

_____

_____

_____

_____

_____

DAY 23

Come to Me

My Glorious Ones,

*W*hatever you are feeling, come to me. Run to me. Rest in me. Rejoice in me. Cry out to me with your deepest longings. I will satisfy your soul. Pour out to me your dreams and visions. I will inspire and empower you. I will nurture and nourish you. I will give you both peace and strength for whatever lies before you. Dwell with me in my presence, where you are vibrant and alive and teaming with endless possibilities. Send your roots to the stream and your branches to the sky. I will strengthen you at your core. I will establish you, adding rings to your "trunk." You are a mighty oak, rooted and established in love, in power, and in strength.

A WORD FOR TODAY

"They are like trees
planted by streams of water,
which yield their fruit in its season,
and their leaves do not wither.
In all that they do, they prosper."

—PSALM 1:3

TODAY'S PRAYER

Dear God,

There are so many things that compete for our attention. There are so many voices that try to lead us to become what others want us to be. Help us avoid the trap of trying to meet the expectations of others. Let us settle into our true beings and come home to ourselves. We are all exquisite originals. Not one of us was created to be a cheap knockoff of someone else. Let us look to you, God, for our sustenance so that we might persevere in becoming whoever we are uniquely created to be.

**Dwell with me in my presence,
where you are vibrant and alive and teaming
with endless possibility.**

QUESTIONS FOR REFLECTION

1. Who do I run to when I am struggling? Where do I go when I need support? In what ways might I try to distract myself from what I am really needing?

    _____

    _____

    _____

    _____

2. Do I have daily habits of reflection, prayer, and/or worship that strengthen my roots and allow me to be sustained by the Creator and or creation itself?

    _____

    _____

    _____

    _____

DAY 24

Dance

My Glorious Ones,

*I*t is time to take yourself less seriously and move without hesitation toward living your life fully. You have been so limited by the constraints that others have put on you and your fear of what others might think. You've sat on the edge of your life and wondered what it would feel like to jump in fully, without fears or insecurities. And now it is time. Don't wait any longer to squeeze every bit of joy that you can from your beautiful life. I am calling you to the middle of the dance floor. Lose yourself in the music. Sing at the top of your lungs. Let go of your inhibitions. Forget how you might look and allow yourself to be free. Open up and live full throttle. Dance and jump and spin and shout with joy. Others will soon join in. They are likely waiting for someone to take the lead.

A WORD FOR TODAY

"Sing to the LORD, sing praises to God;

tell of all God's wonderful works.

Glory in God's holy name;

let the hearts of those who seek the LORD rejoice.

Seek the LORD and God's strength;

seek the LORD's presence continually."

—1 CHRONICLES 16:9-11 (AUTHOR'S PARAPHRASE)

TODAY'S PRAYER

Dear God,

Loosen our chains and free us from being enslaved to the expectations of others. Free us from fear and performance-driven behavior. Let us rejoice in the beautiful lives you have given us. When we are hurting, give us the strength to stand. Fill our hearts with song. When we are in times of rejoicing, let us bring others into the dance. Make us fully alive. Lighten our loads. Even in our grief and pain—especially in our grief and pain—let us spin and turn and shake and quake. Free our bodies from our burdens, and let us actively release what holds us captive and burdens our hearts.

Don't wait any longer to squeeze every bit of joy that you can from your beautiful life.

QUESTIONS FOR REFLECTION

1. Do I follow the instincts and passions that originate inside me, or do I wait to see what others will do?

   _____

   _____

   _____

   _____

2. Do I need others to walk alongside me in order to take risks, or am I willing to do things solo?

   _____

   _____

   _____

   _____

DAY 25

Shine Light

My Glorious Ones,

You have been so deeply indoctrinated into a set of beliefs that you often cannot even recognize it. I implore you to take your own blinders off and shine light into the darkness. I am doing a new thing, and it requires your attention. You shall not be dominated or afraid anymore. Your voice will not stay quiet. You will not be relegated to the margins. I did not put my spirit in you in order that you would feel a sense of lack. It is time to speak truth and stand your ground. You will not need to fight for influence; you possess it already. But you must stop giving your power away. Start pushing back against the oppression and abuse that plagues your culture. It is not from me. I won't stand for it any longer, nor will I tolerate those who want to associate my name with their own thirst for power. If you open your eyes, you can use your wisdom and insight to dismantle the oppression people are facing. Pay attention and start to intervene. Raise your children to know the difference between love and lack. Warn them against hierarchical systems that seek to squelch their spirits. Ensure their wings have a safe place to dry and that they know the heights to which they were meant to fly. Do not let anyone stand in their way. Teach them to discern who is really on their side. It is your responsibility to ensure that your sisters and your children and all those who have been historically marginalized on Earth have a clear path to become all that I have created them to be. Do not be complicit any longer to the powers that keep them at bay. It is time for all of my creation to become empowered. And those who are not helping the meek to rise will fall.

A WORD FOR TODAY

"You are the light of the world.

A city built on a hill cannot be hidden.

People do not light a lamp and put it under the bushel basket;

rather, they put it on the lampstand,

and it gives light to all in the house.

In the same way, let your light shine before others,

so that they may see your good works and give glory

to your God in heaven."

—MATTHEW 5:14–16 (AUTHOR'S PARAPHRASE)

TODAY'S PRAYER

Dear God,

Give us the strength and courage we need to stop tolerating the intolerable.

Ensure that your sisters and your children and
all those who have been historically marginalized
on Earth have a clear path to become all that I
have created them to be.

QUESTIONS FOR REFLECTION

1. Are there people in my life whose need for power or control overshadows their ability to love others without prejudice?

   _____

   _____

   _____

   _____

2. Do I ignore, rationalize, or make excuses for others when their behavior is inexcusable? Does this make me complicit?

   _____

   _____

   _____

   _____

DAY 26

Serve the World with Your Whole Self

My Glorious Ones,

*T*he world needs you. Your sisters need you. And the way you meet this need might be different than you previously believed. You might have been taught to serve, to listen, to learn how to be the best women and wives and mothers you can be. But for many of you, believing this was the "best" way to serve has kept you silent and small. What the world needs most is your voice. What is missing is your perspective. Every time you allow yourself to stay silent, an opportunity to weave beauty into the world is missed. You have tender compassion for those who are misunderstood or marginalized. But you are complicit every time you allow others to dialogue, pontificate, or perpetuate rhetoric that continues to uphold the systems and narratives that keep them enslaved or oppressed. Your silence creates and sustains inequity. Don't ignore the influence you have inside your circle. You can be a voice for those outside your circle. And you have the power to erase circles altogether and help unite us with one another. Simply speaking *your truth will change your current ecosystem and accepted narrative. It will force those around you to look beyond their limited spheres that are populated only with people who look like them and talk like them. Stop nodding along to avoid conflict. Break their bubble so they can see the beautiful community of humans that live outside it. Do not enable them to continue seeing from only their limited perspectives simply because you are afraid to speak up. What are you afraid of? If you lose anything for speaking your truth, you had nothing to begin with.*

A WORD FOR TODAY

"Better is a little with righteousness
than large income with injustice."

—PROVERBS 16:8

TODAY'S PRAYER

Dear God,

Let us see with your eyes and hear with your ears. Let our hearts break for the things that break your heart. Let us see you in all humans and fight for, not against, those who are living alongside us here on Earth. Use us as vessels that will make us a community that communes in unity. Use us as instruments to help humanity remember how to be human. Let us stop yelling and stop closing our ears. Help us embrace and encourage intelligent discourse as a path to peace.

If you lose anything for speaking your truth, you had nothing to begin with.

QUESTIONS FOR REFLECTION

1. How willing am I to see things from multiple perspectives? How often do I empathize and engage with other viewpoints?

   _____

   _____

   _____

   _____

2. What, if anything, keeps me from verbalizing a counterview or introducing a different angle, narrative, or framework into conversations with my family and friends?

   _____

   _____

   _____

   _____

DAY 27

Breathe

My Glorious Ones,

*I*t grieves me to see you being hard on yourselves. I wish you could see what I see when I look at you. You are so precious to me. Everything you say, everything you do, and all that you are blesses my heart. And yet you put so much pressure on yourself to say the right thing, do the right thing, and be the right way. I wish you could let go of the control you think you are supposed to have and receive the joy and life that I have for you. I wish you could remember the light you had in your eyes as a child and find it again. Everything that feels overwhelming is actually a manifestation of your own need for control. When I gaze at you, I am simply delighted with what I see. You are mine, and there is nothing you could do that would ever make me love you more. Likewise, nothing you do could ever make me love you less. Breathe deeply of my love. Take it into your lungs. Know that I made you, and everything I have made is good.

A WORD FOR TODAY

"Jesus said to them again, 'Peace be with you. As God has sent me, so I send you.' When he had said this, he breathed on them and said to them, 'Receive the Holy Spirit.'"

—JOHN 20:21-22 (AUTHOR'S PARAPHRASE)

TODAY'S PRAYER

Dear God,

We are burdened with many worries. Our hearts become drenched in our own pain and suffering. When we struggle, we are overwhelmed. When we are well, we feel the need to do more. There is a weight and measure that feels inherent to the human condition. But in spite of all that feels incomplete, we are inhabited by your face. We are inhabited by your breath. We are inhabited by your peace. Fill up the empty places that only you know exist. Satisfy our deepest longings and heal the wounds of our hearts. Let us drink from your well so that our souls might be healed. Whatever feelings arise today, let us rest in the reality of your love for us and our love for one another.

Know that I made you, and everything I have made is good.

QUESTIONS FOR REFLECTION

1. What are my underlying needs or desires that might manifest themselves as a need or desire for control?

    _____

    _____

    _____

    _____

2. Am I able to tell my sisters what I need, or do I desire to look like I am in control?

    _____

    _____

    _____

    _____

DAY 28

Flow Freely

My Glorious Ones,

There is a song inside of you that needs to be played. There is a picture that needs to be painted. There is clay ready to take its shape that can only do so in your hands. There is a lyric or a poem or a chapter that only you can write. There is a dance unique to the pull in your toes and the music playing in your head. You have unique beauty to weave into the world. Let nothing hinder your progress. Open the floodgates of your creativity. Break the dam that is holding everything inside. You were made to create. It doesn't matter what you produce or who you share it with. The process of being a creator makes you whole. It is where your spirit is free to commune without constraints. It is where I am and where you can know me best. Don't try to understand it, justify it, or quantify it. Just embrace your creativity and live fully open. The waterfall does not wonder if the river upstream will dry up. It just pours itself over the rocks at various speeds and velocities. Regardless of the melt or precipitation, whether a trickle or thunderous roar, it reflects immense beauty just the same. Even a drip is not held back. Likewise you must flow. Don't set up for yourself a dam at your own headwaters. Flow freely and hold nothing back.

A WORD FOR TODAY

"In the beginning
God created . . ."

— GENESIS 1:1 (NIV)

TODAY'S PRAYER

Dear God,

Perhaps the worst thing we have done to one another is to believe the lie that beauty can be defined. We have bought into a culture that creates an ideal that we have come to accept as normal. And yet, the more we try to become like one another, the more we fail at becoming our unique selves. Help us be like children again, who play and paint and build castles in the sand. Help us inspire each other to be as different as possible. Help us rejoice in wanting one another to thrive. Help us outshine our current selves and find safety with friends who call out the deepest and purest places in us. Let us fight for one another's souls and not give up the search for our truest selves. Let us find communion in the deepest places of our hearts.

Open the floodgates of your creativity.

QUESTIONS FOR REFLECTION

1. What creative activities do I find therapeutic, whether I think I am good at them or not?

    _____

    _____

    _____

    _____

    _____

2. What activities make me lose track of time when I am doing them?

    _____

    _____

    _____

    _____

    _____

DAY 29

Take Courage

My Glorious Ones,

𝒴ou have everything you need to face whatever is before you today. At some point in time, you received the message that you have to change or be different in order to overcome your challenges. But there are so many lies built into this message. First of all, I love you as you are. Nothing about you needs to be different from my perspective. But there may be things in your environment that are not best for you. You might have taken up residence in a place that is not your true home. But hear me now: You have limitless strength and courage at your disposal. You are made of resilience and power. You are mine, after all, and I am not just with you. I am in you. Embody the courage that is waiting there, right inside of you. It is ready for you to grab it. Stand up. Walk away from whatever is binding you. Run toward the deepest calling of your heart. You are not feeble or weak. Do not be paralyzed by fear or follow paths set before you by others. They are not you; their journey is theirs. Your life is yours and yours alone. Live it out loud.

A WORD FOR TODAY

"Be strong and courageous; do not be frightened or dismayed, for the LORD your God is with you wherever you go."

—JOSHUA 1:9

TODAY'S PRAYER

Dear God,

Help us take ownership of the courage we already possess. Let us support one another as we face our battles so that no woman feels like she is standing alone on the front lines of her life. Help us summon courage and strength in each other instead of telling others what to do. Thank you for giving each of us what we need for our own path. Let us see the deep potential in our mothers and sisters and daughters. Let us be witnesses to their individual power and strength and be among those who help them move toward their true selves. Grant us collective power and strength to stand up in the face of injustice and dismantle systems of oppression. Help us put shame, judgment, comparison, and isolation behind us so that we can walk together when we feel feeble and afraid. Give all our sisters around the world a deep awareness of who they are and who they might become.

Walk away from whatever is binding you. Run toward the deepest calling of your heart.

QUESTIONS FOR REFLECTION

1. What messages did I receive as a child that might have given me the false
    impression that I am weak or needing to be different than I am? Are there any
    messages that I still believe now?

    _____

    _____

    _____

    _____

2. What challenges have I overcome in the past that provide tangible proof of my
    courage, my strength, and my resilience? How ready am I to tap in daily to
    these attributes?

    _____

    _____

    _____

    _____

DAY 30

Seek and Ye Shall Find

My Glorious Ones,

*O*ne of the greatest gifts in life is to be heard and seen and known; to be surrounded by a tribe, a community, and a family that honors all that is in you and from you. Your heart needs to be spoken. If you find this difficult, it is not because there is something wrong with you. It reflects the inability of those around you to fully appreciate you. You are beautiful and precious, a seeker and speaker of truth. Find people who acknowledge and appreciate you, who long to hear you and see you and know you, who yearn for the connection and authenticity that you also seek. Continue to look for them, and do not stop short. Nurture the relationships that bring you more fully into being and be willing to let go of those that do not.

A WORD FOR TODAY

"Ask, and it will be given to you; search, and you will find;

knock, and the door will be opened for you."

—MATTHEW 7:7

TODAY'S PRAYER

Dear God,

The woes of our culture have come between those of us who are elders. We have become a generation that follows the voices of people instead of our own voice. Differences of opinion and political agendas have served their purpose to divide and destroy us as sisters. Please help us to see clearly and not be duped any longer. Let us fully see our sisters. Open our ears to hear one another's stories. Our lives are not cut and dried. We all harbor both wounds and wisdom. We have much to learn from one another, but only if we are humble and compassionate and willing. Let us not make the choices we have made for decades, choices that honor only our fathers and husbands and authorities, sometimes denying both our own pain and triumphs. Let us speak our truths and make the choices our daughters and granddaughters need us to make. Let us live to empower their lives and the lives of future generations. Let us remove the barriers that might stand in their way.

You are beautiful and precious, a seeker and speaker of truth.

QUESTIONS FOR REFLECTION

1. Do the women in my circle fully know me, embrace me, and extend grace to me?

   _____

   _____

   _____

   _____

2. Are there women outside of my circle who I want to know better? How am I seeking relationships with women who possess the traits I want to develop in myself?

   _____

   _____

   _____

   _____

DAY 31

Relish Each Moment

My Glorious Ones,

Have you begun to notice all the beauty I have set before you? Can you begin to absorb the extravagance of your life on Earth? Are you ready to embrace the joy that is yours to behold? As you awaken, remember you open your eyes to a new world each morning. Some things you can always depend on: the birdsong through your window, the color of the sky changing as the new day dawns, the fresh breath of the breeze. These I will always send as a love song from my heart to yours. But look for me in new ways. I am a generous lover. I am pouring out my love for you in ways that you will only experience if you can slow down and enjoy each part of your day. Take it all in. Relish it all. Life is a beautiful display of my glory for those who take the time to enjoy it.

A WORD FOR TODAY

"Arise, shine, for your light has come,

and the glory of the LORD has risen upon you."

—ISAIAH 60:1

TODAY'S PRAYER

Dear God,

Help us to see your beauty in our world. We are often discouraged or diminished or distracted. Help us to slow down, to look others in the eye, to see the clouds form in the air, to watch the squirrels scurry about the trees, and to notice how the seasons subtly change with the new day. Let us breathe deeply of your love and be restored once again to the peace, power, and dignity that is ours to take up according to your promises and our inheritance as your beloved daughters.

Life is a beautiful display of my glory for those who take the time to enjoy it.

QUESTIONS FOR REFLECTION

1. What pictures come to mind when I consider these proclamations?
    - I have arisen.
    - I shine.
    - My light has come.
    - The glory of the Lord shines upon me.

    _____

    _____

    _____

    _____

2. What do each of these proclamations look like? What do they feel like? What would I be doing if I believed these statements? How would I be living?

    _____

    _____

    _____

    _____

DAY 32

Find Your Deepest Treasure

My Glorious Ones,

F or so long you have looked outside of yourself for answers. You have sought the opinions of others in order to find your own truth. Even the church has perpetuated this stance, making you believe that I am far off and that it is only through study of the Word, perpetual prayer, and gathering in groups with like-minded people that you will be able to hear my voice. Can I tell you something? I am your innermost being. I am the beat in your heart and the breath of your lungs. Just as an artist pours something of themself into each and every creation, all that you are is a reflection of me. You are my heir and my kin. We share DNA. So when people tell you that you need to seek the truth, remember that you hold the truth within your being. Not even your most beloved mentors and leaders can speak into your soul the way that I can. They can only tell their own story. They might have some things in common with you, but they do not know you like I do. Listen and know. I have sown my Word into the depths of your soul. All the wisdom and understanding you need is already within you, like a treasure trove waiting to be opened. Behold the riches I have for you in the quiet places.

A WORD FOR TODAY

"If you love me, you will keep my commandments.
And I will ask God, and God will give you another Advocate,
to be with you forever. This is the Spirit of truth, whom the world
cannot receive because it neither sees God nor knows God.
You know God because God abides with you,
and God will be in you."

—JOHN 14:15–17 (AUTHOR'S PARAPHRASE)

TODAY'S PRAYER

Dear God,

Make us instruments of peace. Help us sow love. Pour the oil of gladness over our souls. Redeem us from the pits set before us and those we set for ourselves. Repattern us after your grace. Rework our neuropathways to be open to things unseen. Rewrite our histories and heal our hearts. Let us lean fully into all we are created to be.

All that you are is a reflection of me.

QUESTIONS FOR REFLECTION

1. Do I trust my own mind, heart, and gut to make decisions and live my life, or do I look outside myself for answers?

   _____

   _____

   _____

   _____

   _____

2. How could my heart, mind, body, and soul serve as my own personal guides?

   _____

   _____

   _____

   _____

   _____

DAY 33

Walk into Your Promise

My Glorious Ones,

I want you to know that I see you, I know you, and I am delighted with what I find when I gaze upon you! Look at how your story is unfolding! Look at the beauty breaking open from your soul! For so long you have been distracted from all that is pure and true and holy, thinking that what mattered most was what others saw in you. You have used all your energy to manage perceptions instead of being your whole, true self. Now that you are willing to let all that go, your true beauty can emerge. Don't get me wrong. The truth is sometimes ugly. It is raw and messy and doesn't fit neatly into a box. But neither do I. And neither do you. And the whole world is breaking open as my children begin to see themselves in my true light. I am ready for you to see. I am ready for you to receive. I am ready to do a new thing. And you are becoming ready too.

A WORD FOR TODAY

"Surely, this commandment that I am commanding you today
is not too hard for you, nor is it too far away. It is not in heaven,
that you should say, 'Who will go up to heaven for us and get it for
us so that we may hear it and observe it?' Neither is it beyond the
sea, that you should say, 'Who will cross to the other side of the sea
for us and get it for us so that we may hear it and observe it?'
No, the word is very near to you; it is in your mouth
and in your heart for you to observe.

See, I have set before you today life and prosperity,
death and adversity. If you obey the commandments of the
LORD your God that I am commanding you today, by loving the
LORD your God, walking in God's ways, and observing God's
commandments, decrees, and ordinances, then you shall live and
become numerous, and the LORD your God will bless you
in the land that you are entering to possess."

—DEUTERONOMY 30:11–16
(AUTHOR'S PARAPHRASE)

TODAY'S PRAYER

Dear God,

Help us to walk into the promises you have for us. Let us choose the path of life and turn our backs from the power and the grip that death and destruction have had on us. Let us stand in unwavering faith and walk with those who will come with us toward your truth and your glory revealed.

The whole world is breaking open as my children begin to see themselves in my true light.

QUESTIONS FOR REFLECTION

1. How would I describe the space I am sitting in right now? What do I see? What do I hear? What do I smell? How does it make me feel?

    _____

    _____

    _____

    _____

2. When I take time to sit quietly, what do I notice that I might usually miss? How does it feel to slow down and take in the present moment?

    _____

    _____

    _____

    _____

DAY 34

Rejoice

My Glorious Ones,

You have awakened to a new dawn. The world brims and bursts with possibility. You are moving forward into a new phase of your life. The past will not haunt you as it once did. But neither should you lean too heavily into the future. You have heard it said, "Do not worry about tomorrow," but I say do not worry about what will happen even ten minutes from now. Attend fully to this present moment. Drink in all that is around you right now. You don't need to plan or premeditate how your day will go. You don't have to be prepared for multiple possibilities. Just live your life in each moment. Take everything in. Whatever you are doing, lean fully into that and that alone. When you rest, let your mind be at ease. When you walk, do so one step at a time. The road will move beneath you, but your gift is the here and now.

A WORD FOR TODAY

"Rejoice in the Lord always; again I will say, Rejoice.
Let your gentleness be known to everyone. The Lord is near.
Do not be anxious about anything, but in everything by prayer and
supplication with thanksgiving let your requests be made known to
God. And the peace of God, which surpasses all understanding, will
guard your hearts and your minds in Christ Jesus.

Finally, brothers and sisters, whatever is true, whatever is honorable,
whatever is just, whatever is pure, whatever is pleasing, whatever is
commendable, if there is any excellence and if there is anything
worthy of praise, think about these things."

—PHILIPPIANS 4:4–8

TODAY'S PRAYER

Dear God,

*Make us an instrument of peace. Sing through us a song of peace. Paint through
us a portrait of peace. Like clay in the hands of the potter, form us and shape
us into vessels filled and overflowing with peace. Let us know the deep riches
of your peace and dwell deeply in it. Transform our hearts and disentangle us
from the noise of the world. Let us engage in the present moment, taking in
the miracle of the magnificent world around us and beholding the exquisite
individual beauty of the fellow humans we encounter and engage with today.*

Whatever you are doing, lean fully into that and that alone.

QUESTIONS FOR REFLECTION

1. How much energy do I spend thinking about the interactions or events
    throughout the day that discourage or disrupt me?

    _____

    _____

    _____

    _____

2. What are the things and who are the people that are bringing me life?

    _____

    _____

    _____

    _____

3. How can I be strengthened by meditating on what is good, pure, joyful, hopeful, and holy in my personal world?

_____

_____

_____

_____

_____

DAY 35

Don't Lose Hope

My Glorious Ones,

I long for you to experience the freedom that I have for you. It is what I made you for. Your freedom, your beauty, and your joy are my delight. I watch you wrestle with the chains that your culture, your history, and your relationships have put upon you. I know their heavy weight upon your back. I know how they have robbed you of your voice. I see you trying to cut yourself loose. You know deep down you were not made for captivity. But in exhaustion and confusion you wonder if you deserve them; you rationalize their existence, or you give up hope of things ever being different. I tell you, do not stop fighting. Do not give up. It is for freedom that I have set you free. I have given you the keys. Take them and begin to open all the locks.

A WORD FOR TODAY

"For surely I know the plans I have for you, says the LORD, plans for
your welfare and not for harm, to give you a future with hope.
Then when you call upon me and come and pray to me,
I will hear you. When you search for me, you will find me;
if you seek me with all your heart."

—JEREMIAH 29:11–13

TODAY'S PRAYER

Dear God,

*It is easy to get discouraged and overwhelmed, especially when we are in pain or
deeply present with and aware of the pain around us. Give us hope and vision
to allow us to keep pushing forward to the days that are ahead. Let us put up a
hand to our oppressors and stop them in their tracks. Let us declare freedom for
ourselves and our sisters, and let no one rob us of that right.*

It is for freedom that you have been set free.

QUESTIONS FOR REFLECTION

1. Can I notice when I start to get discouraged or overwhelmed?

    _____

    _____

    _____

    _____

2. How can I liberate myself today in order to walk in hope, peace, freedom, and joy?

    _____

    _____

    _____

    _____

DAY 36

You Are Known

My Glorious Ones,

I *see your courage, your tenacity, and your strength. It grows more every day. I recognize where you have tried to change the patterns that have been destructive for you in the past. I know when you feel victory in that battle and when it feels as if you have lost the fight. I see the times you have been able to flow, to ride safely through the currents of a beautiful river, and then get safely to the other side. I have also seen you when you have had to fight against rapids to swim upstream and barely keep your head above the water. In all of this, you might not see your progress. But the progress is not in how far you have traveled through this river. The progress is in the strength you have built while doing it. And I will heal you and deliver you. In fact, I have done it already.*

A WORD FOR TODAY

"Before Isaiah had gone out of the middle court, the word of the LORD came to him, 'Turn back and say to Hezekiah prince of my people: Thus says the LORD, the God of your ancestor David: I have heard your prayer, I have seen your tears; indeed, I will heal you; on the third day you shall go up to the house of the LORD. I will add fifteen years to your life. I will deliver you and this city out of the hand of the king of Assyria; I will defend this city for my own sake and for my servant David's sake.'"

—2 KINGS 20:4-6

TODAY'S PRAYER

Dear God,

Strengthen us in our challenges and allow us to know our own strength. Do not allow us to act as feeble ones in need of rescuing. You have given us everything we need to stand up in adversity. But help us to know when to stay and when to go. You call us to pass through and walk through, not to stay in situations that are harmful or toxic. Give us the courage to arrive at the riverbank that is on the other side of our trials. Let us lock arms with one another when we feel weak. May we help our collective sisters remember that we have everything we need to overcome everything that we face. Do not let us succumb to the power of the waves that feel overwhelming; instead, let us rise up and move toward what is good and pure and lovely and true.

I will heal you and deliver you.
In fact, I have done it already.

QUESTIONS FOR REFLECTION

1. When have I demonstrated strength, courage, and wisdom to overcome challenges in my past?

    _____

    _____

    _____

    _____

    _____

2. Do I tend to want others to rescue me, or do I believe I have what I need to move myself away from people, choices, or circumstances that are detrimental to me?

    _____

    _____

    _____

    _____

DAY 37

Burst Forth

My Glorious Ones,

I absolutely delight in you. I find so much joy in communion with you. I am enthralled by your beauty and your life and your light, and I want to blow my breath upon you. You are like glowing embers surrounded by kindling, waiting to burst into vibrant flames. It will only take a moment, but once that moment comes, you will not be able to put the fire out. No one will. You and I will never forget what it took to arrive at this place, but the time is now ripe. I have gathered around you everything you need. The wood is finally dry. It is easily combustible and ready to be consumed in vibrant dancing flames. The time is right. The world is ready. And you are ready to see and embrace and embolden a new day. I am coming in new and powerful ways. I am bursting on the scene. Some will see me right away. Others will deny my presence. When you speak your truth, some will listen and others will rebuke you. Some will adhere to the spirit, and some will turn away in fear. They will listen only to the voices that perpetuate their own narratives. Either way, I will prevail. For both my glory and my wrath uproot foundations of stone like a relentless hurricane in the night. I will clear Earth of the idols man has made and make room on the land and in the hearts of my people. Never again will they wonder. Never again will they fear. My mighty love and power will prevail. I will unearth the rotted roots from the deep recesses of Earth. I will remove the rotted flesh from the tombs. I will purify the streams and the rivers and the lakes and the seas. Even the air will taste sweet as it passes by your lips. I will create a great swell of my spirit. Even the clouds will declare my majesty in broad daylight. I am coming. And when I do, I will restore the beauty of my people from the ground up.

A WORD FOR TODAY

"For I am about to create new heavens

and a new earth;

the former things shall not be remembered

or come to mind."

—ISAIAH 65:17

TODAY'S PRAYER

Dear God,

Let us not be limited by our own understandings. Let us not be harbored by our own breakwalls or weighted down by anchors. Fill us with wonder and curiosity. Let us bask in the unraveling of all we think we understand. Let us gaze into the light of our unknowing.

I am enthralled by your beauty
and your life and your light.

QUESTIONS FOR REFLECTION

1. What if I could imagine a perfect world? What would it look like? What would it sound like? What would it smell and taste like?

    _____

    _____

    _____

    _____

    _____

2. If I woke up in a perfect, glorious, problem-free world, what would I find myself doing today?

    _____

    _____

    _____

    _____

DAY 38

Take Steps

My Glorious Ones,

*G*one are the days when you would look for someone else's footsteps to follow. *Gone is your need to find validation in those who walk before you. Finally, you are seeing that the path I am laying out for you is for you alone. And it is new every day. Each night I come like the ocean to sweep over the footprints in the sand, leaving it flat and perfect and ready for you to be the very first one to encounter it. Feel the way your toes walk upon it as if it has never been trodden on. Feel the soles of your feet sink into it and leave a fresh imprint. Each morning is a new adventure. Do not hold tightly to the course that you think is laid out for you. Do not rely on the plans you think you should follow. Do not expect wisdom and guidance to be laid out in advance for the future. This day is new. It is a bright, white canvas waiting for your paint. Be awake. Be alive. Pay attention to the vastness of the ocean and your unique place on the shore. You have never been exactly at this spot before, and you will never be here again. Don't miss it.*

A WORD FOR TODAY

"Your word is a lamp to my feet and a light to my path."

—PSALM 119:105

TODAY'S PRAYER

Dear God,

Thank you for this one unique and beautiful day. Thank you for the people who we will meet and the stories that will be woven in with ours. Allow us to be in awe of the beauty of every story. Give us the joy of watching our life and the lives of others unfold before us. There is a mighty swell rising. Your people are on a journey. We are like a confluence, a convergence of creeks, which become streams and then rivers. It is all coming together. We cannot see where we are going, but we are noticing how many of us are walking in the same direction. There is no stopping what lies ahead. Help us press toward what we cannot understand but know we cannot deny.

Each morning is a new adventure.

QUESTIONS FOR REFLECTION

1. Where do I see momentum building toward freedom in myself and others?

    _____

    _____

    _____

    _____

2. What is one small thing I can do today to keep moving on the path toward liberation?

    _____

    _____

    _____

    _____

3. What trail am I creating for those who follow behind me?

_____

_____

_____

_____

_____

DAY 39

Live from Your Truth

My Glorious Ones,

A time is coming when everything will be reconciled, and all will be at peace. But for now, standing up for what is right is more important than staying quiet. You must not be complicit to the injustices you see in the world, especially when it comes to the way your sisters are still being dominated across the globe and in your very midst. You must not let your silence be mistaken for agreement with bad behavior. Telling the truth is sure to bring conflict; it always does. But you should not be afraid of dissonance and discord. Be afraid of the ways the world would be robbed of your influence if you chose to stay bound and tied up in your fear of how others will perceive you. Live from your integrity. Live from your truth. Stand up for the oppressed and speak out against the bondage that holds them in place. Love is not afraid of the truth. Light is not afraid of the dark. You are not doing anyone any favors by staying small and hidden. It is time for you to stand up and fight.

A WORD FOR TODAY

"Do not rejoice over me, my enemies;

when I fall, I shall rise;

when I sit in darkness,

the LORD will be a light to me."

—MICAH 7:8

TODAY'S PRAYER

Dear God,

We pray for our enemies and for those who persecute us. We know that no one with flesh and bones can strip us from our knowledge of who we are as your daughters. Yet we can be deeply wounded by bad behavior. It can dissuade us from being our full selves and walking in our own truth. Let us not be ashamed of our stories so that we can crack open the gates of the prisons that have kept us isolated from our sisters and our world. Let us burst forth in light and life and have courage to face whatever each day brings. Bring us the strength, encouragement, and energy to speak the words we need to say today. Let us be present with every moment, waiting for the unfolding of your glory while stepping into it all at the same time.

Love is not afraid of the truth.
Light is not afraid of the dark

QUESTIONS FOR REFLECTION

1. When conflicts arise, how much time and energy do I spend trying to rationalize or justify my behavior? How easy or difficult is it to speak my own truth and feel my honest emotions?

    _____

    _____

    _____

    _____

2. What if I could imagine a life where I do not spend any time or energy analyzing, trying to understand, rationalizing, or justifying the behavior of others? How would my life and my outlook change if I could release other people's behavior and solely focus on being myself?

    _____

    _____

    _____

    _____

DAY 40

Grieve Not for Tomorrow

My Glorious Ones,

Grieve the past. Reflect honestly about what you have been through. Feel the pain of yesterday—all your disappointments, your misgivings, your unmet hopes and dreams. Recognize and honor the many devastations that burdened your heart but didn't steal your soul. In the early hours of the morning, let your tears come. Let your body shake and expel and express the sorrow that it feels from your own experiences and your empathic pain for those around you. Acknowledge what you have been through and what your sisters face across the world today. Consider what you have lost or never had to begin with. Take whatever time you need to give grief its due respect. But then rise to this new day. Set your feet upon the ground and stand up into your calling. Give birth to a new life that is grounded in joy and becoming. Hold tightly to this truth: what is within you far outweighs what is against you. Have courage. Speak truth. Lean into joy—and believe in yourself again.

A WORD FOR TODAY

"Blessed is she who trusts in the LORD,

whose trust is the LORD.

She shall be like a tree planted by water,

sending out her roots by the stream.

She shall not fear when heat comes,

and her leaves shall stay green;

in the year of drought she is not anxious,

and she does not cease to bear fruit."

—JEREMIAH 17:7-8 (AUTHORS PARAPHRASE)

TODAY'S PRAYER

Dear God,

We wait for the revelation of your glory on Earth. In the meantime, we proclaim healing and hope over our lives. We ask you to fill us with the joy of this moment. Let us sing and dance and paint and plant and find productive work with our hands. Let each day be as wet clay in our hands. Let us think and write and speak. Let us listen and hear and absorb. Weave a web between each of us and our sisters. Rip us from isolation and bind us to one another in community. Open the doors of our homes and our hearts to the downtrodden and oppressed. Grant us life and light and joy infused by the smiles and laughter of those we love. Help us lean deeply into the mystery of faith and release our inmost inhibitions. Make us whole. Make us holy. Amen.

**Hold tightly to this truth:
what is within you far outweighs
what is against you.**

QUESTIONS FOR REFLECTION

1. What new truths have I learned throughout my journey that I might not have known without having challenges?

   _____

   _____

   _____

   _____

2. What advice would I give to my younger self?

   _____

   _____

   _____

   _____

3.   What legacy do I want my life to leave for the women who come after me?

_____

_____

_____

_____

_____

_____

_____

_____

_____

_____

_____

_____

ABOUT THE AUTHOR

Jody Tucker is a mother, aunt, teacher, speaker, and author. She holds a bachelor's degree in Human Development from Boston College, a master's in Curriculum and Instruction from Colorado Christian University, and a doctorate in Leadership for Educational Equity from the University of Colorado Denver. She has over three decades of experience in youth ministry, non-profit management, public education, and academia. Jody loves to travel, spend time with her family, be immersed in nature, learn continually, and inspire others to live fully and love well.

CPSIA information can be obtained
at www.ICGtesting.com
Printed in the USA
LVHW060721150223
739506LV00011B/40